Smoke

Smoke

---

poems by
Dorianne Laux

BOA Editions, Ltd.   Rochester, NY   2000

08   09   10   7   6   5

For information about permission to reuse any material from this book please contact
The Permissions Company at www.permissionscompany.com or e mail permdude@eclipse.net

Publications by BOA Editions, Ltd.—a not-for-profit corporation
under section 501 (c) (3) of the United States Internal Revenue Code—
are made possible with the assistance of grants from
the Literature Program of the New York State Council on the Arts,
the Literature Program of the National Endowment for the Arts,
the Sonia Raiziss Giop Charitable Foundation, the Eric Mathieu King Fund
of The Academy of American Poets, The Halcyon Hill Foundation,
as well as from the Mary S. Mulligan Charitable Trust,
the County of Monroe, NY, and from many individual supporters,
and the Estate of E. M. K.

See Colophon on page 72 for acknowledgement of special individual supporters.

Cover Design: Daphne Poulin-Stofer
Typesetting: Richard Foerster
Manufacturing: McNaughton & Gunn, Lithographers
BOA Logo: Mirko

Library of Congress Cataloging-in-Publication Data

Laux, Dorianne.
    Smoke : poems / by Dorianne Laux.-- 1st ed.
        p. cm. -- (American poets continuum series ; vol. 62)
    ISBN 1–880238–85–3 -- ISBN 1–880238–86–1 (pbk.)
        1. Women--Poetry I. Title. II. Series.

PS3562.A8455 S66 2000
895.1'--dc21

                                                                        00-057945

BOA Editions, Ltd
Nora A. Jones, Executive Director/Publisher
Thom Ward, Editor/Production
Peter Conners, Editor/Marketing
Glenn William, BOA Board Chair
A. Poulin, Jr., Founder (1938-1996)
250 North Goodman Street, Suite 306
Rochester, NY 14607
www.boaeditions.org

NATIONAL
ENDOWMENT
FOR THE ARTS

State of the Arts

NYSCA

"*There is no smoke without a fire.*"
　　　　　—Plautus, *Curculio* 1.53

"*Where there's smoke, there's fire.*"
　　　　　—popular saying

"*To want the world is fire; to obtain it, smoke.*"
　　　　　—Tzigane saying

"*She showed me the air and taught me how to fill it.*"
　　　　　—Janis Joplin, of Bessie Smith

CONTENTS

for my daughter, Tristem,
Queen of Everything

 SMOKE

SMOKE

Who would want to give it up, the coal
a cat's eye in the dark room, no one there
but you and your smoke, the window
cracked to street sounds, the distant cries
of living things. Alone, you are almost
safe, smoke slipping out between the sill
and the glass, sucked into the night
you don't dare enter, its eyes drunk
and swimming with stars. Somewhere
a Dumpster is ratcheted open by the claws
of a black machine. All down the block
something inside you opens and shuts.
Sinister screech, pneumatic wheeze,
trash slams into the chute: leftovers, empties.
You don't flip on the TV or the radio, they
might muffle the sound of car engines
backfiring, and in the silence between,
streetlights twitching from green to red, scoff
of footsteps, the rasp of breath, your own,
growing lighter and lighter as you inhale.
There's no music for this scarf of smoke
wrapped around your shoulders, its fingers
crawling the pale stem of your neck,
no song light enough, liquid enough,
that climbs high enough before it thins
and disappears. Death's shovel scrapes
the sidewalk, critches across the man-made
cracks, slides on grease into rain-filled gutters,
digs its beveled nose among the ravaged leaves.
You can hear him weaving his way
down the street, sloshed on the last breath
he swirled past his teeth before swallowing:
breath of the cat kicked to the curb, a woman's
sharp gasp, lung-filled wail of the shaken child.
You can't put it out, can't stamp out the light

and let the night enter you, let it burrow through
your infinite passages. So you listen and listen
and smoke and give thanks, suck deep
with the grace of the living, blowing halos
and nooses and zeros and rings, the blue chains
linking around your head. Then you pull it in
again, the vein-colored smoke,
and blow it up toward a ceiling you can't see
where it lingers like a sweetness you can never hold,
like the ghost the night will become.

LAST WORDS

for Al

His voice, toward the end, was a soft coal breaking
open in the little stove of his heart. One day
he just let go and the birds stopped singing.

Then the other deaths came on, as if by permission—
beloved teacher, cousin, a lover slipped from my life
the way a rope slithers from your grip, the ocean
folding over it, your fingers stripped of flesh. A deck

of cards worn smooth at a kitchen table, the jack
of spades laid down at last, his face thumbed to threads.
An ashtray full of pebbles on the window ledge, wave-beaten,
gathered at day's end from a beach your mind has never left,

then a starling climbs the pine outside—
the cat's black paw, the past shattered, the stones
rolled to their forever-hidden places. Even the poets

I had taken to my soul: Levis, Matthews, Levertov—
the books of poetry, lost or stolen, left on airport benches,
shabby trade paperbacks of my childhood, the box
misplaced, the one suitcase that mattered crushed

to nothing in the belly of a train. I took a rubbing
of the carved wings and lilies from a headstone
outside Philadelphia, frosted gin bottles
stationed like soldiers on her grave:

The Best Blues Singer in the World
Will Never Stop Singing.

How many losses does it take to stop a heart,
to lay waste to the vocabularies of desire?
Each one came rushing through the rooms he left.
Mouths open. Last words flown up into the trees.

BOOKS

You're standing on the high school steps,
the double doors swung closed behind you
for the last time, not the last time you'll ever

be damned or praised by your peers, spoken of
in whispers, but the last time you'll lock your locker,
zip up your gym bag, put on your out-of-style jacket,

your too-tight shoes. You're about to be
done with it: the gum, the gossip, the worship
of a boy in the back row, histories of wheat and war,

cheat sheets, tardies, the science of water,
negative numbers and compound fractions.
You don't know it yet but what you'll miss

is the books, heavy and fragrant and frayed,
the pages greasy, almost transparent, thinned
at the edges by hundreds of licked thumbs.

What you'll remember is the dumb joy
of stumbling across a passage so perfect
it drums in your head, drowns out

the teacher and the lunch bell's ring. You've stolen
A Tree Grows in Brooklyn from the library.
Lingering on the steps, you dig into your bag

to touch its heat: stolen goods, willfully taken,
in full knowledge of right and wrong.
You call yourself a thief. There are worse things,

you think, fingering the cover, tracing
the embossed letters like someone blind.
This is all you need as you take your first step

toward the street, joining characters whose lives
might unfold at your touch. You follow them into
the blur of the world. Into whoever you're going to be.

DEATH COMES TO ME AGAIN, A GIRL

Death comes to me again, a girl in a cotton slip.
Barefoot, giggling. It's not so terrible, she tells me,
not like you think: all darkness and silence.

There are wind chimes and the scent of lemons.
Some days it rains. But more often the air
is dry and sweet. We sit beneath the staircase
built from hair and bone and listen
to the voices of the living.

I like it, she says, shaking the dust from her hair.
Especially when they fight, and when they sing.

RAY AT 14

Bless this boy, born with the strong face
of my older brother, the one I loved most,
who jumped with me from the roof
of the playhouse, my hand in his hand.
On Friday nights we watched *Twilight Zone*
and he let me hold the bowl of popcorn,
a blanket draped over our shoulders,
saying, Don't be afraid. I was never afraid
when I was with my big brother
who let me touch the baseball-size muscles
living in his arms, who carried me on his back
through the lonely neighborhood,
held tight to the fender of my bike
until I made him let go.
The year he was fourteen
he looked just like Ray, and when he died
at twenty-two on a roadside in Germany
I thought he was gone forever.
But Ray runs into the kitchen: dirty T-shirt,
torn jeans, pushes back his sleeve.
He says, Feel my muscle, and I do.

ABSCHIED SYMPHONY

Someone I love is dying, which is why,
when I turn the key in the ignition
and the radio comes on, sudden and loud,
something by Haydn, a diminishing fugue,
then back the car out of the parking space
in the underground garage, maneuvering through
the dimly lit tunnels, under low ceilings,
following yellow arrows stenciled at intervals
on gray cement walls and I think of him,
moving slowly through the last
hard days of his life, I won't
turn it off, and I can't stop crying.
When I arrive at the tollgate I have to make
myself stop thinking as I dig in my pockets
for the last of my coins, turn to the attendant,
indifferent in his blue smock, his white hair
curling like smoke around his weathered neck,
and say, Thank you, like an idiot, and drive
into the blinding midday light.
Everything is hideously symbolic:
the Chevron truck, its underbelly
spattered with road grit and the sweat
of last night's rain, the Dumpster
behind the flower shop, sprung lid
pressed down on dead wedding bouquets—
even the smell of something simple, coffee
drifting from the open door of a café;
and my eyes glaze over, ache in their sockets.
For months now all I've wanted is the blessing
of inattention, to move carefully from room to room
in my small house, numb with forgetfulness.
To eat a bowl of cereal and not imagine him,
drawn thin and pale, unable to swallow.
How not to imagine the tumors
ripening beneath his skin, flesh

I have kissed, stroked with my fingertips,
pressed my belly and breasts against, some nights
so hard I thought I could enter him, open
his back at the spine like a door or a curtain
and slip in like a small fish between his ribs,
nudge the coral of his brain with my lips,
brushing over the blue coils of his bowels
with the fluted silk of my tail.
Death is not romantic. He is dying. That fact
is stark and one-dimensional, a black note
on an empty staff. My feet are cold,
but not as cold as his, and I hate this music
that floods the cramped insides
of my car, my head, slowing the world down
with its lurid majesty, transforming
everything I see into stained memorials
to life—even the old Ford ahead of me,
its battered rear end thinned to scallops of rust,
pumping grim shrouds of exhaust
into the shimmering air—even the tenacious
nasturtiums clinging to a fence, stem and bloom
of the insignificant, music spooling
from their open faces, spilling upward, past
the last rim of blue and into the black pool
of another galaxy. As if all that emptiness
were a place of benevolence, a destination,
a peace we could rise to.

STAIRWAY TO HEAVEN

We're deep into the seventh hour, the car
packed with electric guitars and pint-size
speakers, skateboards and fishing rods,
crumpled copies of *Thrasher* and *Mad*.
Ray is riding shotgun—he and Dan switched
at the last stop as agreed. One minute
they're yelling every cussword they know
out the open windows, the forbidden syllables
swept beneath the tires of trucks; the next,
they're asleep and dreaming, bare toes
twitching, their shaved heads lolling
on the torn upholstery. But now,
Dan's reading by flashlight and Ray's
looking out at the river, skipping through
stations on the radio when he hears
"Stairway to Heaven"
and freezes, snaps his head around
to each of us, his mouth open
in the absolute O of exquisite luck.
We listen to the guitar bend out its solo
and everyone's still. The train
straining up the tracks beside us. The moon
hauling its great solitude into the sky.
Ray turns up the volume, closes his eyes, says,
Doesn't this part give you the chills?
We nod in agreement, then settle again
into our separate worlds. In mine
I'm beholden to any boy brave enough
to be stunned, to sit still and hushed
while the grievous tones wash through him
like dusk. Stars flicker in the ether—headlights
fog-mired—cornfields buried in mist.
The Siskiyou Mountains divide up ahead,
waiting to swallow us whole.

EVEN MUSIC

Drive toward the Juan de Fuca Strait.
Listen to "Moondog Matinee."
No song ever written gets close to it:

how it feels to go on after the body
you love has been put into the ground
for eternity. Cross bridge after bridge,

through ten kinds of rain, past
abandoned fireworks booths,
their closed flaps streaked with soot.

Gash on the flank of a red barn:
Jesus Loves You. 5 $ a Fish.
He's dead. Where's your miracle?

Load a tape into the deck so a woman
can wear out a love song. Keep moving,
keep listening to the awful noise

the living make.
Even the saxophone, its blind,
unearthly moan.

TRYING TO RAISE THE DEAD

Look at me. I'm standing on a deck
in the middle of Oregon. There are
people inside the house. It's not my

house, you don't know them.
They're drinking and singing
and playing guitars. You love

this song. Remember? "Ophelia."
Boards on the windows, mail
by the door. I'm whispering

so they won't think I'm crazy.
They don't know me that well.
Where are you now? I feel stupid.

I'm talking to trees, to leaves
swarming on the black air, stars
blinking in and out of heart-

shaped shadows, to the moon, half-
lit and barren, stuck like an ax
between the branches. What are you

now? Air? Mist? Dust? Light?
What? Give me something. I have
to know where to send my voice.

A direction. An object. My love, it needs
a place to rest. Say anything. I'm listening.
I'm ready to believe. Even lies, I don't care.

Say, burning bush. Say, stone. They've
stopped singing now and I really should go.
So tell me, quickly. It's April. I'm

on Spring Street. That's my gray car
in the driveway. They're laughing
and dancing. Someone's bound

to show up soon. I'm waving.
Give me a sign if you can see me.
I'm the only one here on my knees.

THE WORD

You called it *screwing*, what we did nights
on the rug in front of the mirror, draped
over the edge of a hotel bed, on balconies
overlooking the dark hearts of fir trees

or a city of flickering lights. You'd
whisper that word into my ear
as if it were a thing you could taste—
a sliver of fish, a swirl of chocolate

on the tongue. I knew only
the rough exuberant consonants
of *fucking*, and this soft *s* and hard *c*
was a new sound—querulous, slow,

like the long moments of leaving
between thrusts. I don't know what
to make of it, now that you're gone. I think
of metal eating wood. Delicate filaments

quivering inside a bulb of thin glass.
Harsh light. Corks easing up through
the wet necks of wine bottles. A silver lid
sealed tight on a jar of skinned plums.

I see two blue dragonflies hovering, end
to end, above the pond, as if twisting
the iridescence deep into each other's
body, abdomens writhing, spiraling

into the wing-beaten air. And your voice
comes back to me through the trees, this word
for what we couldn't help but do
to each other—a thin cry, unwinding.

HOW IT WILL HAPPEN, WHEN

There you are, exhausted from another night of crying,
curled up on the couch, the floor, at the foot of the bed,

anywhere you fall you fall down crying, half amazed
at what the body is capable of, not believing you can cry

anymore. And there they are: his socks, his shirt, your
underwear, and your winter gloves, all in a loose pile

next to the bathroom door, and you fall down again.
Someday, years from now, things will be different:

the house clean for once, everything in its place, windows
shining, sun coming in easily now, skimming across

the thin glaze of wax on the wood floor. You'll be peeling
an orange or watching a bird leap from the edge of the rooftop

next door, noticing how, for an instant, her body is trapped
in the air, only a moment before gathering the will to fly

into the ruff at her wings, and then doing it: flying.
You'll be reading, and for a moment you'll see a word

you don't recognize, a simple word like cup or gate or wisp
and you'll ponder it like a child discovering language.

Cup, you'll say it over and over until it begins to make sense,
and that's when you'll say it, for the first time, out loud: He's dead.

He's not coming back, and it will be the first time you believe it.

THE LINE

The line runs the length of the department store aisle—a mother grips a toddler's hand, hugs a baby to her hip, jiggles a newborn's stroller with her foot. Their nappy hair is woven, bright beads and bumpy cornrows. They're in various stages of crankiness. She's trying to find a practical way to fill out the form. She fastens the child's fist to the stroller, instructs her to hold on, shifts the baby to the other hip, balances the clipboard on the crossbar and writes as it teeter-totters above the newborn's head. Behind me a woman speaks to her children in Chinese. When she asks where the forms are I point to the front of the line, offer to watch her kids while she's gone. She fixes their fingers to my shirttails, hands delicate as wrens, skin tinted yellow beneath the brown. I finish filling out my form. I know my daughter's eyes are blue but I reach out, lift her chin, and look again. There is no word for this particular color. We've been here for over an hour, waiting to have our children fingerprinted, birthmarks and scars typed neatly on pocket-size laminated cards, their pictures in the left-hand corner so if they're stolen we'll have this card to show. So we won't be caught with our faces frozen, mouths open, unable to remember when we saw them last, what they were wearing, the exact color of their shoes. We're making our children stand in this line trying not to think about coffins the size of dresser drawers, the dragging of rivers. We're promising them the park later, rides on the plastic ponies out front. We're the mothers of the twentieth century and we stand in line at Payless, waiting to reach the front desk where men from the American Legion will take thousands of thumbs and fingers and press them into a pad of ink, recording the delicate whorls on treated paper. We're gratefully taking each folded towelette to clean the purple stains from their hands as they sit on the stools and smile, as only our children can. As if nothing were wrong in the new world. As if the future were theirs.

WINDOW

Graveyard trees hug their shadows close.
Wind scuffs dirt along the sunken stones.
In the valley below, the carved letters
of your name are gathering moss, your bones
gone to chalk beneath a pot of flowers.
I've wept, graceless, over the stanchioned
rhododendrons, mothers hushing children
as they wandered past. With you I had no pride.
Why should anything change after your death?
I unseal the envelope to your strands of hair,
take one between my lips and pull it through.
The candle's guttered flame has licked
the last of you, eaten the thin wick of your body
that once flared under my hands, scorched
the curtains you once swept open
to let the darkness pour in.

WING

for Miguel Hernández
(1910–1942)

Madrid, 1934

Until a shepherd boy from Orihuela
climbed a tree, curled his bare toes
around a high olive branch, buried his face
among the leaves and whistled, Neruda
had not heard a nightingale.

PRAYER

Sweet Jesus, let her save you, let her take
your hands and hold them to her breasts,
slip the sandals from your feet, lay your body down
on sheets beaten clean against the fountain stones.
Let her rest her dark head on your chest,
let her tongue lift the fine hairs like a sword tip
parting the reeds, let her lips burnish
your neck, let your eyes be wet with pleasure.
Let her keep you from that other life, as a mother
keeps a child from the brick lip of a well,
though the rope and bucket shine and clang,
though the water's hidden silk and mystery call.
Let her patter soothe you and her passions
distract you; let her show you the light
storming the windows of her kitchen, peaches
in a wooden bowl, a small moon of blue cloth
she has sewn to her skirt to cover the tear.
What could be more holy than the curve of her back
as she sits, her hands opening a plum.
What could be more sacred than her eyes,
fierce and complicated as the truth. Your life
rising behind them. Your name on her lips.
Stay there, in her bare house, the black pots
hung from pegs, bread braided and glazed
on the table, a clay jug of violet wine.
There is the daily sacrament of rasp and chisel,
another chair to be made, shelves to be hewn
clean and even and carefully joined
to the sun-scrubbed walls, a small knife
for whittling abandoned scraps of wood
into toys and spoons for the children.
O Jesus, close your eyes and listen to it,
the air is alive with birdcalls and bees,
the dry rustle of palm leaves,

her distracted song as she washes her feet.
Let your death be quiet and ordinary.
Either life you choose will end in her arms.

FIRE

HEART

The heart shifts shape of its own accord—
from bird to ax, from pinwheel
to budded branch. It rolls over in the chest,
a brown bear groggy with winter, skips
like a child at the fair, stopping in the shade
of the fireworks booth, the fat lady's tent,
the corn dog stand. Or the heart
is an empty room where the ghosts of the dead
wait, paging through magazines, licking
their skinless thumbs. One gets up, walks
through a door into a maze of hallways.
Behind one door a roomful of orchids,
behind another, the smell of burned toast.
The rooms go on and on: sewing room
with its squeaky treadle, its bright needles,
room full of file cabinets and torn curtains,
room buzzing with a thousand black flies.
Or the heart closes its doors, becomes smoke,
a wispy lie, curls like a worm and forgets
its life, burrows into the fleshy dirt.
Heart makes a wrong turn.
Heart locked in its gate of thorns.
Heart with its hands folded in its lap.
Heart a blue skiff parting the silk of the lake.
It does what it wants, takes what it needs, eats
when it's hungry, sleeps when the soul shuts down.
Bored, it watches movies deep into the night,
stands by the window counting the streetlamps
squinting out one by one.
Heart with its hundred mouths open.
Heart with its hundred eyes closed.
Harmonica heart, heart of tinsel,
heart of cement, broken teeth, redwood fence.
Heart of bricks and boards, books stacked
in devoted rows, their dusty spines

unreadable. Heart
with its hands full.
Hieroglyph heart, etched deep with history's lists,
things to do. Near-sighted heart. Club-footed heart.
Hard-headed heart. Heart of gold, coal.
Bad juju heart, singing the low down blues.
Choir boy heart. Heart in a frumpy robe.
Heart with its feet up reading the scores.
Homeless heart, dozing, its back against the Dumpster.
Cop-on-the-beat heart with its black billy club,
banging on the lid.

OLYMPIA

I convinced Manet to paint me with a tinge of ocher
in his brush—true color of our world—yellow
of jaundice, syphilis, death,

each line indelicate, flowers messy, spattered
on the canvas, wrapped in the stiff, waxy paper
used to carry home butchered

meat, gutted fish, used later to take the bones
to the trash. And the cat, its salacious eyes wide,
a tom who would risk his life

for sex: ruthless, common, king of the alley. Yes,
I was lower-class, but I had power, an artist myself.
I tied the ribbon around my neck,

to separate the head from the body, to say: This meat
you have tasted, left spread on the sheets as you dress
for the boulevard, tossing

your money on the bed, this is the body you refused
to see: its dirty feet and sallow breasts, its sun-darkened
hands even *maquillage*

can't disguise, I have divided from the mind
which dismisses you, the mouth with its insolent
sneer, the blunt, unrefined chin

held high. Admit it! What you fear are my eyes,
their intelligence twinned: When I die, you are sure
to follow. And the black maid,

you ask, whose arms are burdened with your blossoms
of death, of course, she knows, too. See how she holds
them back even as their faces

tumble forward, toward the hand that will live for centuries. This hand that will never rise from my lap.

THE SHIPFITTER'S WIFE

I loved him most
when he came home from work,
his fingers still curled from fitting pipe,
his denim shirt ringed with sweat,
smelling of salt, the drying weeds
of the ocean. I'd go to where he sat
on the edge of the bed, his forehead
anointed with grease, his cracked hands
jammed between his thighs, and unlace
the steel-toed boots, stroke his ankles
and calves, the pads and bones of his feet.
Then I'd open his clothes and take
the whole day inside me—the ship's
gray sides, the miles of copper pipe,
the voice of the foreman clanging
off the hull's silver ribs. Spark of lead
kissing metal. The clamp, the winch,
the white fire of the torch, the whistle,
and the long drive home.

FIRESTARTER

Since this morning he's gone through
an entire box of Safeway matches, the ones
with the outlines of presidents' faces
printed in red, white, and blue.
He's not satisfied with one match at a time.
He likes to tip the book over the ashtray
and light them up all at once, the flame
less than an inch from his fingertips
while the fathers of the nation burn.
He doesn't care about democracy,
or even anarchy, or the message inside
that promises art school for half price
if he'll complete a woman's profile
and send it in. The street address burns,
ZIP code and phone number, the birth
and death dates of the presidents,
the woman's unfinished face. I'm afraid
he'll do this when I'm not around
to keep him from torching the curtains,
the couch. He strikes match after match,
a small pyre rising from the kitchen table.
I ought to tell him about Prometheus
and the vulture, the wildfires
burning in the Oregon hills.
I want to do what I should
to make him afraid, but his face
is radiant, ablaze with power,
and I can't take my eyes from the light.

THE STUDENT

She never spoke, which made her obvious,
the way death makes the air obvious
in an empty chair, the way sky compressed

between bare branches is more gray or blue,
the way a window is more apparent than a wall.
She held her silence to her breast like a worn coat,
smoke, an armful of roses. Her silence
colored the smaller silences that came and went,
that other students stood up and filled in.

I leaned near the window in my office. She sat
on the edge of a chair. Hips rigid, fidgeting
while I made my little speech. February

light pressed its cold back against the glass,
sealing us in. She focused on my lips
as I spoke, as if to study how it's done,
the sheer mechanics of it: orchestration
of jaw and tongue, teeth shifting in tandem,
shaping the air. So I stopped, let her silence

drift over us, let it sift in like smoke or snow,
let its petals settle on my shoulders.
I looked outside to the branches

of a stripped tree, winter starlings
folded in their speckled wings, chilled flames
shuddering at the tips. Students wandered
across campus as if under water, hands and hair
unfurling, their soundless mouths churning—
irate or ecstatic, I couldn't tell—ready to burn

it all down or break into song. When I looked back
her eyes had found the window: tree, students,
birds swimming by, mute in their element.

It was painful to hear the papery rasp
of her folding and unfolding hands, to watch
color smudging her neck and temple, branching
to mist the delicate rim of one ear. I listened
to the air sunder between us, the feverish hush
collapse. I could hear her breath—smoke

rising from ice. I could see what it cost her
to make that leap. What heat it takes
for the body to blossom into speech.

PEARL

She was a headlong assault, a hysterical discharge,
an act of total extermination.
                —Myra Friedman, *Buried Alive:*
                    The Biography of Janis Joplin

She was nothing much, this plain-faced girl from Texas,
this moonfaced child who opened her mouth
to the gravel pit churning in her belly, acne-faced
daughter of Leadbelly, Bessie, Otis, and the booze-
filled moon, child of the honky-tonk bar-talk crowd
who cackled like a bird of prey, velvet cape blown
open in the Monterey wind, ringed fingers fisted
at her throat, howling the slagheap up and out
into the sawdusted air. Barefaced, mouth warped
and wailing like giving birth, like being eaten alive
from the inside, or crooning like the first child
abandoned by God, trying to woo him back,
down on her knees and pleading for a second chance.
When she sang she danced a stand-in-place dance,
one foot stamping at that fire, that bed of coals;
one leg locked at the knee and quivering, the other
pumping its oil-rig rhythm, her bony hip jigging
so the beaded belt slapped her thigh.
Didn't she give it to us? So loud so hard so furious,
hurling heat-seeking balls of lightning
down the long human aisles, her voice crashing
into us—sonic booms to the heart—this little white girl
who showed us what it was like to die
for love, to jump right up and die for it night after
drumbeaten night, going down shrieking—hair
feathered, frayed, eyes glazed, addicted to the song—
a one-woman let me show you how it's done, how it is,
where it goes when you can't hold it in anymore.
Child of everything gone wrong, gone bad, gone down,

gone. Girl with the girlish breasts and woman hips,
thick-necked, sweat misting her upper lip, hooded eyes
raining a wild blue light, hands reaching out
to the ocean we made, all that anguish and longing
swelling and rising at her feet. Didn't she burn
herself up for us, shaking us alive? That child,
that girl, that rawboned woman, stranded
in a storm on a blackened stage like a house
on fire.

FIGURES

When he walks by an old drunk or a stumbling vet,
he stops to rummage in his pockets for change
or a stray bill, remembers the cold urge
of fifteen years ago that kept his joy trapped
in a bottle or in the stained nub of a roach
passed from one set of cracked lips to another.
Their creased palms open like scrolls
toward the bright coins of light, stamped chips
of winter barter for the scraps and opiates
of this city. He won't ask and doesn't care
what his money is exchanged for: a blanket,
a pair of wrecked shoes, the harsh, sharpened
glare of a needle, or a pack of smokes.
Who can calculate the worth
of one man's pain? What they need, he figures,
can't be more than what he owes.

FEAR

We were afraid of everything: earthquakes,
strangers, smoke above the canyon, the fire
that would come running and eat up our house,
the Claymore girls, big-boned, rough, razor blades
tucked in their ratted hair. We were terrified

of polio, tuberculosis, being found out, the tent
full of boys two blocks over, the kick ball, the asphalt,
the pain-filled rocks, the glass-littered canyon, the deep
cave gouged in its side, the wheelbarrow crammed
with dirty magazines, beer cans, spit-laced butts.

We were afraid of hands, screen doors slammed
by angry mothers, abandoned cars, their slumped
back seats, the chain-link fence we couldn't climb
fast enough, electrical storms, blackouts, girlfights
behind the pancake house, Original Sin, sidewalk
cracks and the corner crematorium, loose brakes
on the handlebars of our bikes. It came alive

behind our eyes: ant mounds, wasp nests, the bird
half-eaten on the scratchy grass, chained dogs,
the boggy creekbed, the sewer main that fed it,
the game where you had to hold your breath
until you passed out. We were afraid of being

poor, dumb, yelled at, ignored, invisible
as the nuclear dust we were told to wipe from lids
before we opened them in the kitchen,
the fat roll of meat that slid into the pot, sleep,
dreams, the soundless swing of the father's
ringed fist, the mother's face turned away, the wet
bed, anything red, the slow leak, the stain
on the driveway, oily gears

soaking in a shallow pan, busted chairs stuffed
in the rafters of the neighbor's garage, the Chevy's
twisted undersides jacked up on blocks, wrenches
left scattered in the dirt.

It was what we knew best, understood least,
it whipped through our bodies like fire or sleet.
We were lured by the Dumpster behind the liquor store,
fissures in the baked earth, the smell of singed hair,
the brassy hum of high-tension towers, train tracks,
buzzards over a ditch, black widows, the cat
with one eye, the red spot on the back of the skirt,
the fallout shelter's metal door hinged to the rusty
grass, the back way, the wrong path, the night's
wide back, the coiled bedsprings of the sister's
top bunk, the wheezing, the cousin in the next room
tapping on the wall, anything small.

We were afraid of clothesline, curtain rods, the worn
hairbrush, the good-for-nothings we were about to become,
reform school, the long ride to the ocean on the bus,
the man at the back of the bus, the underpass.

We were afraid of fingers of pickleweed crawling
over the embankment, the French Kiss, the profound
silence of dead fish, burning sand, rotting elastic
in the waistbands of our underpants, jellyfish, riptides,
eucalyptus bark unraveling, the pink flesh beneath,
the stink of seaweed, seagulls landing near our feet,
their hateful eyes, their orange-tipped beaks stabbing
the sand, the crumbling edge of the continent we stood on,
waiting to be saved, the endless, wind-driven waves.

FAMILY STORIES

I had a boyfriend who told me stories about his family,
how an argument once ended when his father
seized a lit birthday cake in both hands
and hurled it out a second-story window. That,
I thought, was what a normal family was like: anger
sent out across the sill, landing like a gift
to decorate the sidewalk below. In mine
it was fists and direct hits to the solar plexus,
and nobody ever forgave anyone. But I believed
the people in his stories really loved one another,
even when they yelled and shoved their feet
through cabinet doors or held a chair like a bottle
of cheap champagne, christening the wall,
rungs exploding from their holes.
I said it sounded harmless, the pomp and fury
of the passionate. He said it was a curse
being born Italian and Catholic and when he
looked from that window what he saw was the moment
rudely crushed. But all I could see was a gorgeous
three-layer cake gliding like a battered ship
down the sidewalk, the smoking candles broken, sunk
deep in the icing, a few still burning.

TWILIGHT

My daughter set whatever had begun
to wither or rot on the rail
of the backyard deck. Pear, apple, over-ripe
banana, in October a pumpkin
that by August had gone to dust.
She took photos of the process: pear
with its belly bruised, weekly
growing more squat, the dark spot spreading.
Orange caving in at the navel.
Banana skins tanning like animal hides.
As their outsides grew tough,
their insides grew moist— a crack in the crust
and the dank pudding spewed out.
Pear neck at half-mast, pear bottom black,
crease hardened to crevasse, pear neck
sunk into the drooped shoulders of pear.
She observed and recorded the progress, watched
the realm of the solid transmute and dissolve,
documenting the musk-fragrant, incremental
descent, its delectable inevitability.
She delighted in her entropic world
with complete abandon— never expressing
repulsion or remorse, only taking
her deliberate daily photos: pumpkin
with its knifed hat tipped jauntily
above carved eyes, pumpkin sinking sweetly
into its own orange face, buckling, breaking,
sweating in sunlight, mold webbed and glowing
through a triangle nose, the punched-out smile
a grimace slipping down its furred chin.
When did she become disinterested, distracted
by her life? Where to go? What to do?
Did her socks match? One day she left
her dark harvest behind and walked
to the rink where her skate blades

shimmed the ice, inscribing girlish circles
on the blue skirl of the deserted rink.
Or she lingered at the stalls until twilight,
brushing down her favorite horse, sugar
cubes in her pockets, an apple in her purse.
She actually had a purse. Filled to the clasp
with the evidence of her life: lip gloss,
stubby pencils and colored pens, a little book
she wrote in faithfully, archiving last
names that began with A on the A page,
B's on the B, a billfold with money
and a photo ID, her own face gazing out
through the tiny plastic window.
She stared back at herself like any ordinary girl,
not a girl obsessed with ruin and collapse
who stalked her backyard with a camera.
Something else had caught her eye.
See her lift the tawny jewel
to his whiskered lips, her hand level,
her fingers flat and quivering. Look
at the gratitiude in her face
when he takes the first dangerous bite.

ICELAND

Berkeley, California

The girls' bathroom is tiled in pink
up to the shoulder, then yellow paint takes over,
smeared in circles toward a ceiling of pockmarked
slab insulation. Monique unlaces her skates
on the rim of a chipped sink, sloughs off her socks,
leans near the air freshener that reeks fake pine,
hung from rusted brackets, encrusted
with seepage leaked in fern patterns.
Nyeema walks in to wash her hands.
Faucets bleed mineral deposits. Powdered soap
in slogged heaps beneath fuchsia dispensers,
floor black and tacky with cola and gum.
Wobbly hearts and penises unscroll down the walls,
an inky graffiti collage: *Andrea Loves Wesley.*
Myron and June. We own this dive.
Martin was here 2/15/85.
The light switch is stuck, Tampax vendor
stuffed with spit wads in the quarter slot.
Ice skate tips kicked into the walls.
OUT OF ORDER signs on half the stalls.
Locks torn from doors, hinges sprung.
The trick is to lean back, stretch out a toe
to hold it closed, then try to pee.
The bell rings on the rink and girls
squirm through the doors. Wanda
fishes in her bra for a smoke, lights up
in a corner, gray rings breaking to nothing
on the spiderwebbed vent.
Sandy gets her period in stall four
and outside the ice truck scrapes
the chewed rink smooth.
Sharla and Kyanne clap a hand-jive,
slap thighs and knees as the loudspeaker sings

I just called to say I love you.
Melanie knots her slip above the waistband of her skirt.
Aurora lines her lips with an Avon sampler:
Dusty Rose. Barbara jimmies for mirror position,
parts her bangs, slicks them down with spit
and bobbie pins, glares back at the cracked glass.
In the bathroom at Iceland, Clara announces
she might be pregnant, bends over one knee, drops
ladybug dots of red nail polish
onto a run in her tights. Jasmine is crying.
Her dad's new girlfriend hates her.
Darla stops carving FUCK into a door,
slings advice over her shoulder like a clot of wet hair:
Screw her. Who cares? She's not your goddamn mom.
Peregrine twists crust from her pierced earrings.
Tanya repairs an unraveled cornrow
with a glass bead. The bell rings on the rink
and they swing out the doors.
Darla and Doris meet Troy.
Jasmine shows off in new skates, the sequins
on her Dorothy Hamill skirt a constellation
as she spins on thick ice. Monique stays back,
stares out a gap in the chicken-wired windows,
picks at a blister on her heel, peels
the yellow skin away from the pink, and drops
the withered scraps, like petals, into the sink.

REETIKA ARRANGES MY CLOSET

Her apartment is a lesson in schematics.
The bookcase catty-corner in a corner.
Five books per shelf. No knickknacks. No dust.
On the desk a clean sheet of onionskin
fixed with a glass Bluebird-of-Happiness.
One silver pen. One wedge-of-flesh eraser.
I follow her from room to room, ooohing in awe,
windows emitting their glorious scent of Windex,
waxed floors wafting up a slick, lemony, yes.
This is the life, I quip. She sings, Tea?
and before I can answer she's opened the cupboard
to boxes stacked by size, cans in tight rows, spices
hung on the door in all their alphabetized splendor.
She leans against a sink so clean all I can think
is *inner sanctum.* She's a dark star hovering
at the window in her short jet skirt, inky V-neck
T-shirt, ebony sweater vest, sable tights, glassy black
stacked heels trussed at the instep with gold
Monte Carlo buckles. She giggles
through a sweet veil of steam rising
from the rim of her cup, her hair so black
it's blue, feathered into perfect wings.
She offers to help me organize my closet,
to separate my skirts by length and color,
throw out everything that doesn't fit,
box winter sweaters in cedar chips.
I say okay and take her to my house. We ratchet open
the front door, push past stacks of newspapers,
bags of recyclables, magazines and flowerpots—
the everything I've saved. We make our way
to the living room, stand amid its junk and rubble,
baskets and bookcases, pillows spilling
from the overstuffed couch. Photographs
and posters ascend the walls, spiny plants
fall along the sills, their tendrils looped

through narrow crevices between
the paper angels and the waterballs.
She swoons like a schoolgirl holding a ticket
for free admission to the Carlsbad Caverns,
lifts each object up from its circle of dust,
catalogs its history like an archaeologist
uncovering an ancient ruin. This, she squeals,
is great, as we high-step along the clogged hallway
to my bedroom with its four-poster strung
like a great web, the crossbars and knobs draped
with panties, socks, bras, to the closet's open doors
where she stares at the tangled spew of purses,
belts, and shoes. Reetika's oolong eyes are glowing.
Her hands are opening and closing.
I'm going to give her everything I own.

OH, THE WATER

You are the hero of this poem,
the one who leans into the night
and shoulders the stars, smoking
a cigarette you've sworn is your last
before reeling the children into bed.

Or you're the first worker on the line,
lifting labeled crates onto the dock,
brown arms bare to the elbow,
your shirt smelling of seaweed and soap.

You're the oldest daughter
of an exhausted mother, an inconsolable
father, sister to the stones thrown down
on your path. You're the brother
who warms his own brother's bottle,
whose arm falls asleep along the rail of his crib.

We've stood next to you in the checkout line,
watched you flip through tabloids or stare
at the face on the *TV Guide* as if it were the moon,
your cart full of cereal, toothpaste, shampoo,
day-old bread, bags of gassed fruit,
frozen pizzas on sale for 2.99.

In the car you might slide in a tape,
listen to Van Morrison sing *Oh, the water.*
You stop at the light and hum along, alone.

When you slam the trunk in the driveway,
spilling the groceries, dropping your keys,
you're someone's love, their one brave hope;

and if they don't run to greet you or help
with the load, they can hear you,
they know you've come home.

THE GARDENER

Who comes to tend the garden,
the green shoots flowering
into radiant stars, the damp mulch
fragrant—so soft you might think
a body had opened under your shoe.
Who's the gardener here,
the wide-beamed straw-hatted man
who scoops the earth and turns it over,
the root-clumped clod arcing
toward the sun, hovering impossibly
against the sky and then falling, flecks
of black leaf mold and families of ants
sloughing off in its wake—earthbound,
landing close to the hole it was born from.
Who is this man so in love with the turnips,
the tomato vines strung like a harp
against the fence, even the plastic
yellow flags flipping in the wind
that mark this garden his own.
He's pacing the perimeter again,
measuring the bean patch foot by foot,
fingering the intimate flowering peas,
the blowsy cabbage, a rake in one hand,
a heart-shaped spade in the other.
Eden. Gethsemane. Tivoli. No garden
is like his. This is the ground he knows
will bury him, the same moist earth
that feeds his days, clay smoothed
and fired into rough glazed plates
laden with the rain-rich, sun-rich squash
of his succulent life. Pollen and dust
sleep in his forehead's creases, shimmer
in the sweat on the back of his neck.
Seeds jostle in the folds of his socks,
dead leaves curl in his pockets, root hairs

cling to the cuffs of his jeans.
Who is this dank old man, this silly coot,
this foolish greenhouse of a man
whose back wallows in the sun,
who kneels now and digs deep
into the shadow he casts on the soil?

NEON HORSES

(*Artist Martin Anderson built a series of
neon horses which appeared in fields along
the I-5 throughout Oregon.*)

To come upon one, driving toward your lover
in the dark, the highway steaming
under four grooved wheels, the dry hum
of roadside weeds, cigarette smoke's
ribbon wisped out the open wind wing,
radio low, shadow of some small creature
careening alongside the interstate.

To look up and see one grazing in a field,
serene, calm as the moon in the severed dark,
bright hooves sunk in black nightgrass,
head dipped like a spoon to a pool of earth,
delicate spine glowing, blue bridge
arched to the stars, tail stroke throwing off
ghost light, empty haunch through which
the sagebrush, windswept, sways.

To see, for miles, its burning shape,
barest outline of throat, foreleg, the imagined
fetlock brushed in. The surprise of horse
held like breath, horse and what horse means
gleaming like a constellation, lineaments
of the true world: cowbird and sugar cube,
fallen apple, tractor wheel, torn wheat
in its worn treads, silo, hay, the baled sky, ruffled pond
from which geese, squalling, lift.

The after smell of horse, rising, feral,
floating above the sorrel. The way night
knows itself with roses and thorns, buried edges,

knowing his arms are down there, electric, spread,
his jaw lifted to the kiss on its way, depth
to be met and entered, full on his lips, moving toward it,

a still joy hovering behind the eyes:
as when the living horse is seen,
incomparable, massive, universe
of horse, too much for the mind,
only the heart's dark world can hold it,
crucible moment, muscle greeting muscle,
grass, gallop, crushed blossom, intake
of voltage, blue horse of the valley, horse
of dream, lit chimera distilled from liquid air.

THE ORGASMS OF ORGANISMS

Above the lawn the wild beetles mate
and mate, skew their tough wings
and join. They light in our hair,
on our arms, fall twirling and twinning
into our laps. And below us, in the grass,
the bugs are seeking each other out,
antennae lifted and trembling, tiny legs
scuttling, then the infinitesimal
ah's of their meeting, the awkward joy
of their turnings around. O end to end
they meet again and swoon as only bugs can.
This is why, sometimes, the grass feels electric
under our feet, each blade quivering, and why
the air comes undone over our heads
and washes down around our ears like rain.
But it has to be spring, and you have to be
in love—acutely, painfully, achingly in love—
to hear the black-robed choir of their sighs.

LIFE IS BEAUTIFUL

and remote, and useful,
if only to itself. Take the fly, angel
of the ordinary house, laying its bright
eggs on the trash, pressing each jewel out
delicately along a crust of buttered toast.
Bagged, the whole mess travels to the nearest
dump where other flies have gathered, singing
over stained newsprint and reeking
fruit. Rapt on air they execute an intricate
ballet above the clashing pirouettes
of heavy machinery. They hum with life.
While inside rumpled sacks pure white
maggots writhe and spiral from a rip,
a tear-shaped hole that drools and drips
a living froth onto the buried earth.
The warm days pass, gulls scree and pitch,
rats manage the crevices, feral cats abandon
their litters for a morsel of torn fur, stranded
dogs roam open fields, sniff the fragrant edges,
a tossed lacework of bones and shredded flesh.
And the maggots tumble at the center, ripening,
husks membrane-thin, embryos darkening
and shifting within, wings curled and wet,
the open air pungent and ready to receive them
in their fecund iridescence. And so, of our homely hosts,
a bag of jewels is born again into the world. Come, lost
children of the sun-drenched kitchen, your parents
soundly sleep along the windowsill, content,
wings at rest, nestled in against the warm glass.
Everywhere the good life oozes from the useless
waste we make when we create—our streets teem
with human young, rafts of pigeons streaming
over the squirrel-burdened trees. If there is
a purpose, maybe there are too many of us
to see it, though we can, from a distance,

hear the dull thrum of generation's industry,
feel its fleshly wheel churn the fire inside us, pushing
the world forward toward its ragged edge, rushing
like a swollen river into multitude and rank disorder.
Such abundance. We are gorged, engorging, and gorgeous.

NOTES

"Last Words," p. 15: Bessie Smith's epitaph.

"Abschied Symphony," p. 21: The German word *abschied* means "farewell."

"Stairway to Heaven," p. 23: Words and music by Jimmy Page and Robert Plant, performed by Led Zeppelin.

"Trying to Raise the Dead," p. 25: Excerpt from "Ophelia," words and music by Robbie Robertson, performed by The Band.

"Wing," p. 31: Pablo Neruda's literary magazine, *Caballo verde por la poesia*, was one of the first to publish the poems of Miguel Hernández.

"Olympia," p. 39: The French word *maguillage* means "makeup" or "facial powder."

"Iceland," p. 53: Line from "I Just Called to Say I Love You," by Stevie Wonder.

"The Orgasms of Organisms," p. 63: The title is a phrase taken from the poem "Without Form," by Adam Zagajewski.

ACKNOWLEDGMENTS

Grateful acknowledgment is made to the editors of the following journals and anthologies in which these poems or earlier versions of them appeared.

Alaska Quarterly Review: "Death Comes to Me Again, A Girl," "How It Will Happen, When";

The American Poetry Review: "The Gardener," "Ray at 14," "Abschied Symphony", "The Orgasms of Organisms," "Smoke," "Pearl," "Fear," "Neon Horses";

DoubleTake: "The Shipfitter's Wife";

Five Points: "The Student";

International Quarterly: "The Line";

The Kenyon Review: "Prayer," "Firestarter";

Pearl: "Wing";

Ploughshares: "Trying to Raise the Dead," "Family Stories";

Rattle: "Stairway to Heaven";

Red Rock Review: "Iceland";

The Southern Review: "The Word";

Waterstone: "Twilight."

"The Shipfitter's Wife" was included in *The Best American Poetry 1999*, edited by Robert Bly (Scribner, 1999); "The Orgasms of Organisms" was included in *Touch Me There: A Yellow Silk Book* (Warner Books, 1999); "Prayer" received a 1999 Pushcart Special Mention.

My deepest gratitude to Kim Addonizio, Jane Hirshfield, Phil and Fran Levine, Marie Howe, Ellen Bass, Maxine Scates, Jack Gilbert, Doug Anderson, The Archangels: Michael, Mike, and Matthew, The BOA Boys (and girl!), Ray & Dan, my students, my teachers, my family, to Rosen

always, and to Joseph Millar for going the distance. In loving memory of
Al Poulin.

"How It Will Happen, When" is for Stephie Mendel, "Firestarter" is for my
nephew, Ray, "Wing" is for Mike McGriff, "The Gardener" is for Phil and
Fran, "The Orgasms of Organisms" is for Judith and Ruth, "The Student"
is for Rosann, "The Line" is for Polly Klass and the town of Petaluma, "Oh,
the Water" is for my sister, Antoinette.

ABOUT THE AUTHOR

Dorianne Laux is the author of two collections of poetry from BOA Editions, *Awake* (1990) and *What We Carry* (*1994*), which was a finalist for the National Book Critics Circle Award. She is also coauthor, with Kim Addonizio, of *The Poet's Companion: A Guide to the Pleasures of Writing Poetry* (W. W. Norton, 1997). Among her awards are a Pushcart Prize for poetry and a fellowship from The National Endowment for the Arts. Her work has appeared many literary journals, including in *The Harvard Review*, *Alaska Quarterly Review*, *The Southern Review*, *Ploughshares*, *Shenandoah*, *The Kenyon Review*, *The American Poetry Review*, *The Washington Post*, *DoubleTake*, *ZYZZYVA*, and *The Best American Poetry 1999*. She is an associate professor in the University of Oregon's Program in Creative Writing.

BOA EDITIONS, LTD.

AMERICAN POETS CONTINUUM SERIES

Vol. 1   *The Fuhrer Bunker: A Cycle of Poems in Progress*
W. D. Snodgrass

Vol. 2   *She*
M. L. Rosenthal

Vol. 3   *Living With Distance*
Ralph J. Mills, Jr.

Vol. 4   *Not Just Any Death*
Michael Waters

Vol. 5   *That Was Then: New and Selected Poems*
Isabella Gardner

Vol. 6   *Things That Happen Where There Aren't Any People*
William Stafford

Vol. 7   *The Bridge of Change: Poems 1974–1980*
John Logan

Vol. 8   *Signatures*
Joseph Stroud

Vol. 9   *People Live Here: Selected Poems 1949–1983*
Louis Simpson

Vol. 10   *Yin*
Carolyn Kizer

Vol. 11   *Duhamel: Ideas of Order in Little Canada*
Bill Tremblay

Vol. 12   *Seeing It Was So*
Anthony Piccione

Vol. 13   *Hyam Plutzik: The Collected Poems*

Vol. 14   *Good Woman: Poems and a Memoir 1969–1980*
Lucille Clifton

Vol. 15   *Next: New Poems*
Lucille Clifton

Vol. 16   *Roxa: Voices of the Culver Family*
William B. Patrick

Vol. 17   *John Logan: The Collected Poems*

Vol. 18   *Isabella Gardner: The Collected Poems*

Vol. 19   *The Sunken Lightship*
Peter Makuck

Vol. 20   *The City in Which I Love You*
Li-Young Lee

Vol. 21   *Quilting: Poems 1987–1990*
Lucille Clifton

Vol. 22   *John Logan: The Collected Fiction*

Vol. 23   *Shenandoah and Other Verse Plays*
Delmore Schwartz

Vol. 24   *Nobody Lives on Arthur Godfrey Boulevard*
Gerald Costanzo

Vol. 25   *The Book of Names: New and Selected Poems*
Barton Sutter

Vol. 26   *Each in His Season*
W. D. Snodgrass

Vol. 27   *Wordworks: Poems Selected and New*
Richard Kostelanetz

Vol. 28   *What We Carry*
Dorianne Laux

Vol. 29   *Red Suitcase*
Naomi Shihab Nye

Vol. 30   *Song*
Brigit Pegeen Kelly

Vol. 31   *The Fuehrer Bunker: The Complete Cycle*
W. D. Snodgrass

Vol. 32   *For the Kingdom*
Anthony Piccione

Vol. 33   *The Quicken Tree*
Bill Knott

Vol. 34   *These Upraised Hands*
William B. Patrick

Vol. 35   *Crazy Horse in Stillness*
William Heyen

COLOPHON

Smoke, poems by Dorianne Laux, was typeset using
Goudy and Monotype Rococo Ornament fonts
by Richard Foerster, York Beach, Maine.
The jacket and cover were designed by
Daphne Poulin-Stofer, Rochester, New York.
Manufacturing was by McNaughton & Gunn, Saline, Michigan.

Special support for this book came from the following
individuals and organizations:
Debra Audet, Central Oregon Sweet Adelines,
Susan Dewitt Davie, Richard Garth & Mimi Hwang,
Dane & Judy Gordon, Chris & Joanna Hodgman,
Robert & Willy Hursh, George Keithley,
Archie & Pat Kutz, John & Barbara Lovenheim,
Annette Lynch, Boo Poulin,
Deborah Ronnen, Andrea & Paul Rubery,
Pat & Michael Wilder.